For Richard
All the best,
always
CB

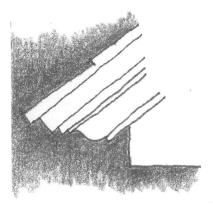

Despite its historical œsthetic,
this is a Shape that *Works*.

Proceeds from the sale of this book go to
The Associates' Fund of the Cooper Union for the
Advancement of Science and Art

THE SHAPE

of.

THINGS.

that.

W O R K

~

The Fourth Architecture

CURTIS B WAYNE
ARCHITECT

Cover design by Caitlin Everett

ISBN-13: 9781490904559
ISBN-10: 1490904557

Foreword

Well now, of course, we know that the superior mind does not learn by comparison, it learns by analysis. The inferior mind will learn by comparing this to that, which is how I guess we got to the old saying that "comparisons are odious." They're not enlightening, they're odious, because you don't get to the truth of anything that way; you simply slip around on the surface. But here, if you get the habit of analysis, and you study a thing for its nature, then come to a decision – that's enlightenment, not conditioning. The conditioned mind will learn by comparison. The enlightened mind will learn by analysis.

– Frank Lloyd Wright

You never change things by fighting the existing reality. To change something, build a new model that makes the existing model obsolete.

– R. Buckminster Fuller

And the basic project of art is to make the world whole comprehensible, all its glory – not through arguments, but through feeling.

– Robert Hughes

Ah, feeling. And that is why architecture is not art.

Contents

I. The Fourth Architecture

An Architecture Without "Style"
The Architecture of Shapes That Work

When architects create shape, *do they do so for form's sake alone?*

In our era of constrained resources, both of materials and of energy, who shall integrate the technologies needed to mediate between the ordinary demands of comfort and the *extra*ordinary aspects of architecture?

Are architects the natural and logical integrators of the artistic with the technical? It can be argued that owing to our training we – above all other professions – "should" be the master builders, the master integrators. But instead we see the profession fractured by the self-identifying trends of so-called sustainability; the intrusion of pure form, driven by the complexities of shape-making made possible by computational generation; and the relegation of discussions of urbanism and social function to the "soft" professions of the social sciences. And yet, we architects can and should include all these aspects in our practice; we *must*, else we are merely makers of decoration.

The First Architecture

In the beginning of western architecture, there was at first the Hellenistic Roman architecture; an architecture of columns and beams – we call this "trabeated." Over the centuries of Roman assimilation of other culture's technologies, the Romans increasingly adopted and perfected the arch, an Etruscan form appropriated by the Romans early in their ascendancy. By the end of the Roman era, in or around the fifth century A.D. the arch and its revolved form – the dome – had supplanted the trabeated style of the original Roman architecture.

ROMAN ARCHITECTURE.

I term this Roman Hellenism the "First" Architecture. But within the evolution of that First Architecture lay the seeds of what would spring forth as the Second Architecture; as domes and arched structures of what we know as *Romanesque* grew to ever larger size in the remnants of the Roman empire, there arose a desire for an expression both evocative of the soaring forests of Northern Europe and suited to harvesting what little daylight was available in the dark of the long winter – harnessed in service to the religious oligarchy of the Church of Rome. This new Second Architecture is what we call Gothic.

And, as the development of the Gothic arose from the late stages of the Roman, the next architecture arose from the dematerializing effect of the late Gothic – whose soaring pointed arches presaged the artistic flourishes of the late-19th century *Art Nouveau* – as well as the architecture of dematerialized mass that we call Modern – and which I call the Third Architecture. And the dematerialized clerestories of the Gothic cathedral also presage the glass house of the Modern era.

So, after a thousand years of Gothic and its resonant revivals, and a couple of centuries of the "Modern" – the Third Architecture (both architectures of dematerialization) – there is now the time for a Fourth Architecture – freed of formal style, an architecture that serves both beauty *and* utility. We are too wise, too adept, and too responsible to continue making forms for the sake of "sculpture you can live in" – like this clumsy building:

Astor Place "Sculpture you can live in."
Gwathmey Siegel Architects, 2005

—— formed for the sake of creating a "style." A sculpture you can *live* in? Really now? An orthopædic fitting, more like!

If we do not make form that is beautiful because it
performs a function of light, heat, cooling, and clean
air; provides acoustic delight (isolation such that one
does not hear one's neighbor's noise and scuffle) and
of thermal, ergonomic and economic comfort – then
we have shirked our responsibilities as the primary Integrators. And that is exactly what the 21st century
architect's role must be.

If we do not integrate all of these aspects of building,
we are no longer the *archi*-tects, we are decorators.
For – an architect operates at the highest level of both
technician and artist; in our training and practice we,
above all other disciplines, have a measured and a
learned ability to manage all the countless tradeoffs,
compromises, and countervailing necessities to serve
economy and beauty, function and form.

This, then, is the goal of the Fourth Architecture.

It is easy to find examples of shapes that do NOT work; that is because the failures are plentiful – and cautionary. Examples in the positive column are fewer; success of integration of functional form with the beautiful is as elusive as is wishing for a conclusive definition of beauty itself.

One example of an exemplary failure: early in the twenty-first century a building for a small college in New York City was designed that *could* have been Fourth Architecture – but, alas, its functional elements do *not*, in a real and practical sense, *work*. It is worthy to examine the failures, revealing a key element of Fourth Architecture, which is the avoidance of excessive degrees of complexity and an over-reliance on advanced and expensive technologies.

The building in question is the mundanely-named New Academic Building at the Cooper Union for the Advancement of Science and Art, at the intersection of Third and Fourth Avenues in New York City, by Thom Mayne of Morphosis Architects, completed in 2009, the college's sesquicentenary year.

Features that *might have* worked include social elements; sustainable *gestures;* and untenable "greenwash" – the use of inappropriate technologies, such as the building's co-generation system, which produces huge amounts of heat that cannot be used and commonly is turned into domestic hot water, which a classroom and lab building scarcely requires. Let me identify a few other failures.

Fraudulent "Function"

At first glance, what attracts attention is the perforated stainless steel screen that wraps an otherwise unremarkable glass and aluminum curtainwall office block. This screen is *supposed* to be an *operable* shading device, mitigating solar heat gain – and, by means of operable panels in the screen admit more sunlight to reach the curtainwall, for solar heat gain in winter. Or, if in conditions of excessive solar heat, these panels were to open to allow heat trapped and created by convection currents – to escape.

41 Cooper Square – the New Academic Building
Showing the vents that most assuredly do not work.

Additionally, operable window sash in the curtainwall immediately behind these screen panels are *purportedly* able to be operable to provide natural ventilation. The problem is: these screen panels do not open – therefore they block the operable sash; the screens are controlled by a computer data and sensing system that has never worked, and still doesn't – now four years after substantial completion – and probably

14

never shall. Photographs that show these panels in an open position are promotional shots; for those photos the panels were operated manually.

So then let us quickly review the shape of some buildings whose form is an expression of their functional responses to site, climate and appropriate technology. *Shapes that work.*

The Glaxo Wellcome building in Greenford, UK has double walls of glass, which temper the effects of solar exposure. Simple enough – and effective. Note also the *horizontal* sun shades, which also serve as reflecting light shelves. This is a feature we shall see quite prevalently in the future – in Fourth Architecture, *because it works.*

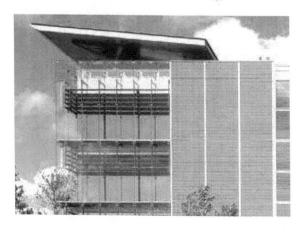

Glaxo-Wellcome, Greenford UK RMJM Architects

15

This is a splendid example of the Fourth Architecture. But this use of glass and metal need not be "Modern," in the "International Style" of the dematerializing sense of modernism.

An example of a style-less structure, attractive – because it works – is architect George Fred Keck's Crystal House at the 1934 Chicago "Century of Progress" World's Fair. It is a building that reveals its structure, has glass walls that provide passive solar heating, and has operable shading devices.

The exposition also saw introduction of Fuller's Dymaxion car (the outline of which we see above in the Crystal House garage.)

The Crystal House "inhabitants" salute from the roof of the carport, as inventor R Buckminster Fuller offers the ladies a ride in his Dymaxion Car.

But Fourth Architecture need not be entire buildings; the economy of ergonomic organization and convenience is characteristic of Fourth Architecture. Here's a fitting, yet ingeniously modest example – the "Frankfurt kitchen" in which everything is conveniently at hand, clean and organized:

Designed by Margarete Schütte-Lihotzky, the Frankfurt Kitchen was introduced in the Ginnheim- Höhenblick Housing Estate, Frankfurt-am-Main, Germany, 1926 – 27.

One last major building I would have you consider is the Helicon building, an office development in London EC2A, designed by Sheppard Robson Architects.

Its facades "look" as they do as a result of environmental features. Note especially that the south-facing walls are generally double-walled curtain-wall, and that sun shades are not of the "eyebrow" type popularized by le Corbusier, but are rather horizontal and thin, working as both shades and light shelves to bounce daylight into the building, as

we previously noted at the Glaxo Wellcome building.

To look at one more example – from quite awhile back – in the stylistic middle-years, between the Gothic and the Modern eras, we see glimpses of the Fourth Architecture.

Here are architectural features that are both beautiful and that work:

Sir John Soane's breakfast room, circa 1824.

This intersection between a peripheral clerestory and a domed room at Sir John Soane's home and museum in Lincoln's Inn Fields, London, introduces daylight that highlights his *objets d'art and* enhances the spatial delight of the ceiling.

II. What Were They Thinking?

Really - what were *they* thinking? *This is* funny, *isn't it? It is an entrance to an* underground *platform for an* elevated *funicular tramway.*

"Daddy, why does it look like a mushroom?"

Do you, as an interested lay-person, often encounter a building and wonder "what in heaven's name were they thinking when they designed *that*?" Or perhaps you are a recent design school graduate – or a newly licensed architect – and wonder the same yourself.

When we design buildings, are we creating *form for form's sake?* or: do we create and choose a form that *does* something, that interacts with the senses in a discernable and *identifiable* fashion?

Does the form we create *interact with nature and site* in a way that gives value to the whole of the structure – in a way that improves the quality of life for those humans occupying the structure?

Might we, by the examination of the architectures that have preceded our current time help us discern *how we might do better?*

These thoughts, in sum, describe the questions posed by examining The Shape of Things That Work.

But first, a little scholarship is in order, for without some analysis of the matters at hand, we are merely *comparing*, which Mr. Wright insists is inferior to analysis.

III. The Scholarly Stuff

Let us, for the sake of argument, posit that architecture is the synthesis of all arts, all sciences, and of all physical and perceptual human experiences; and – moreover – that architecture is an attempt at formal solutions in *service of improving the quality of life.*

When we architects give life to form, apply form to mere *building* with the intention of imbuing the work with *beauty* – do we have *reasons* for the forms we choose? Are we sculptors of buildings, decorators; or are we problem solvers? Technicians or artists? All or none of the above?

R. Buckminster ("Bucky") Fuller once remarked *"When I am working on a problem I never think about beauty. I only think about how to solve the problem – but when I have finished, if the solution is not beautiful, I know it is wrong."* [1]

His argument, then, is fundamental to these essays – that to find some measure of beauty, or rightness of form, we must gain discernment by analyzing the shapes and forms that are not only beautiful, but beautiful in their utility; forms that *solve problems.* Forms that are more than forms for their own sake. Architectural forms that are more than art; Fourth Architecture.

The Elusive Spirit of Beauty

My mentor and teacher, the architect-poet John Q. Hejduk argued:

"The fundamental issue of architecture is that does it affect the spirit, or doesn't it? If it doesn't affect the spirit, it's building. If it affects the spirit, it's architecture." He went on to say *"An architecture doesn't necessarily mean that it's the final form of a built building; a drawing, to me, is a completed piece of architecture, a building is a completed piece of architecture, a photograph of a drawing or a photograph of a(n) architecture is a piece of architecture. Each act is individually an act of architecture."* [2]

And from that we can – because we *must* – recapture the essence of architectures that engage the spirit – *and*, most important – serve to elevate the quality of life.

It can be argued that art, on the other hand, cannot be *useful* – because then it is commercial, or merely craftwork. Architecture that is primarily art therefore cannot be useful. *Where is the genius of the architect's role as* the *prime integrator of all technologies, all needs, all uses in the paradigm of architecture-as-art?*

Without this integration, this service to humankind, architects merely become aesthetes and others – less well trained – will decide how our built environment is formed.

Let these essays then, on our current state of architecture, be understood as *an act of architecture*,
an offering to the spirit of architecture, *and* an examination of spirit, imbued with natural meaning.

But, how *do* shapes and form work to improve or to
impoverish the human spirit in ordinary life?

Quality and Meaning

Why are our recent architectural wonders so
marked by their emphasis purely on visual form and
not on utility, or function? What is the cumulative
effect of buildings whose primary reason to *be* is to
be novel? Where is meaning? Where is quality of
thought made real in comfort, economy and utility?

In 2012 Sir David Chipperfield, the Director of the
13th Venice Biennale of Architecture had this to say
on the matter:

*"Architecture has to have meaning, not just novelty.
The biggest ambition can't be just to be different.
When we only talk about what architecture looks
like, its colour or what's in the lobby we are just becoming decorators. We have lost confidence in our
ability to really do things. The conversation has become too introverted. How come there is such a
disconnect between what architects think they are
doing and how they wish to serve society and how
they really serve society?. All good architects think
they are making a contribution to society: why does*

society think architects are just a bunch of profiteer-ing egotistical joyriders?" [3]

On a macro level, why do millions of us live no bet-ter than we did 40 or 100 years ago – our houses' air quality as poor as when we cooked on coal-burning stoves; our outdoor air worse than in the days of wood-burning fireplaces? Is it the density of our cities? If so, what excuse is there for grandiose buildings that exalt the ego of the bad actors on the stage of our landscape, seeking to achieve a degree of notoriety, effectively saying: "Look at this grand structure, isn't it *marvelous*, are we not su-perb leaders? Isn't our taste superior?"

Utility and Beauty

The thesis of Fourth Architecture is that the shape of buildings should *do* more than be visually stimulat-ing. This is, of course, a value judgment. *Why* this *should* be so is a philosophical proposition, and a very old proposition at that.

"Socrates writes in Pistias *that the beautiful (euryth-mon) in relation to a purpose is superior to the beautiful in itself. From these two statements, one thing is clear: A new formal attitude toward design was born, and the question of whether forms are normative in themselves – that is, autonomous – became an issue."* [4]

"The Question of Autonomy in Architecture" from which this is cited argues that this marks the transi-tion in western, Hellenistic thought from mystical or

27

religious rules of order and form – to the rational urge to integrate form with useful utility. So I am scarcely original in this regard. Who amongst us is sufficiently Sophist to argue with Socrates?

Other Antecedents

Eugene Emmanuel Viollet-le-Duc, in his essays "Discourses on Architecture" declares:

"Art, therefore, must be recognized as one of the elements of (French) civilization; and if this civilization is on the broad road, not of decline, but of progress, her arts should naturally be in a flourishing condition; if they are not, the misfortune can only be attributed to the artists. Now, as regards architecture, I am convinced that we are far behind the times. In this respect we are just at the point where the West was in the time of Galileo in regard to science. Those who consider themselves the guardians of the eternal principles of beauty would gladly shut up, if they could, as a dangerous madman, any one who should undertake to demonstrate that such principles are independent of any particular form of expression, and that there is no reason why, because the principles are invariable, these forms should remain eternally unchanged and confined to certain traditional rules governing all detail and proportion." [5]

So what *are* the reasons that directed and informed how and what we built in ages past? What lessons can be re-learned? Should we even look to the past, when our current technologies are so superior, so sublime, so advanced?

The Chicago architect Louis Sullivan penned this famous sentiment in 1896:

"It is the pervading law of all things organic and inorganic, of all things physical and metaphysical, of all things human and all things superhuman, of all true manifestations of the head, of the heart, of the soul, that life is recognizable in its expression, that form ever follows function. This is the law." [6] Emphasis by Sullivan in the original text.

Handmaiden to utility is a belief in structural honesty. In 1971 the Philadelphia architect Louis Kahn argued that structure should be revealed and self-evident, writing:

"The structure of the room must be evident in the room itself. Structure, I believe is the giver of light. A square room asks for its own light to read the square. It would expect the light either from above or from its four sides as windows or entrances." [7]

Formal bias

Certain radical modernists (member of CIAM – see below) of the early 20th century thought that we should not look to the past; for them, the past was marked by centuries of war, of unparalleled poverty, of pestilence. For them, a total break from history was not only a matter of inventive necessity;

29

it was also a political statement against monarchy and plutocracy, in favor of liberal ideas of freedom, expressed in new forms not beholden to tradition or historical habit.

In this sentiment I find resonance, but also a failure in method for failing to carry forward basic knowledge inextricably tied to history.

For example, the mid-twentieth century students of Walter Gropius – one of the founders and for a time the director of the legendary art school "Bauhaus" in Dessau, Germany – were not taught architectural history, and in many schools of architecture still, students are in total ignorance of the profession's recent experiments, successes and failures, carried out in the spirit of this modernist break from history; and therefore, are doomed to repeat cartoon versions of cartoon reiterations of ideas once well-meant, novel in their time, but which may not actually work, and whose appeal to the spirit has faded.

I frequently encounter recent architecture school graduates who know nothing about Brutalism; the Post-WWII social housing experiments carried out by Peter and Alison Smithson; or the architectural evangelism of CIAM (the early 20th century Congrès Internationaux d'Architecture Moderne – influential proponents of "International Style" modernism.)

What does it matter, might you say? We have trained barbarians, if we have not trained future architects with *discernment* to know what works and what does not *work.* "*We are left being no more than decorators*"[8] This is not the prejudice of the author; the noted architect Sir David Chipperfield said this.

Continuing in the spirit, if not the substance, of the Gropius/Bauhaus "out with history" approach to architectural design is a new(-ish) strain of computer-generated formalism, whose chief proponent calls it:

"Parametricism"

—— which is proclaimed to be a new emerging *style* of architecture. Its proponents are Patrik Schumacher and his partner, the British-Iranian architect Zaha Hadid.

COURTESY ZAHA HADID ARCHITECTS

So, you might say: What is wrong with computer-generated, purely algorithm-driven form making? Isn't that scientific? It certainly is modern, in that such forms could never have been created before the advent of cheap computing power. Isn't it wonderful *to create* novel *shapes? Isn't that* progress?

I strenuously argue that what has resulted is a *decorative* style that begets a *place-less-ness,* free of any relationship to site, and certainly *willfully* ignorant of the patterns of use, of human habit, of comfort, or of ease. The result is a cohort of buildings that could – and are – be found in Paris or New York or on the shore of Lake Michigan or in the deserts of the United Arab Emirates; therefore, buildings that are everywhere – and nowhere, created for no place in particular, and have nothing to do with where they've been plopped down, like so many Martian invasion vehicles.

So this is not my argument for a return to Neo-Classicism, nor to "traditional" forms – unless they be traditional and functional – but rather for creating and choosing architectural Shapes That Work. In our architecture my goal is to indentify demonstrable solutions for improving the lives of those people who live in, work in, or visit the buildings for which we are responsible, and have a long-term impact on our landscape.

But there *are* those (q.v: Dr Peter Eisenman) who will, and do, say that the purpose of architecture is *only* to create structures that elevate the spirit with form alone, irrespective of utility or function. That architecture is not a charitable enterprise, and cannot possibly engage issues of the common good in the ordinary sense of the quality of individual life, but only and most emphatically the common and communal life through our contemporary temples of culture: our museums, the residences of the most economically favored, and our office towers – themselves, to adapt the jingoistic language and thought of Franklin W Woolworth – being our current-day "cathedrals of commerce."

I refute the ego-monument-makers. I denounce their works as simply more of the "bread and circus" diversions of the Roman Empire. (Not an original thought; see Manfredo Tafuri's "Architecture and Utopia: Design and Capitalist Development," MIT 1976.) For indeed, ours is an empire of capital that far exceeds the reach, if not the grasp, of that late empire, over two millennia past.

I urge the recapture of *reasoned* form, an approach founded on the making of shapes that provide a function, in service to the quality of life of the individual.

In closing, let us consider what Viollet-le-Duc had to say about architectural discourse as he encountered it in the mid-nineteenth century:

"Here for four hundred years we have been disputing about the relative value of ancient and modern art, and during all that time our discussions have turned, not upon essential principles, but upon quibbles and equivocations, upon details and principles, upon the authority for this, that, or the other form.

"The result is that we architects, absorbed in an art half science and half sentiment, have succeeded in developing for the public only certain mysterious hieroglyphics which they cannot possibly understand, and so they let us wrangle among ourselves in the empty vanity of our exclusiveness.

"Shall we never have our Moliere to treat us as he did the physicians of his time? We too have our Hippocrates and Galen; must we harp on them forever?" [(9)]

A drawing by Viollet-le-Duc, showing his synthesis of Medieval fantasy and 19th c. technology

Viollet-le-Duc, bound by his time in history has it *almost right* if one compares his times with ours – as he continues, saying:

"I am ready to agree with anyone that pure invention is not necessary to architecture; that the duty of architects is not to create, but to analyze, combine and appropriate the traditionary (sic) forms at their disposal; that the art is so imperious concerning the means of execution, that we must take all the elements of design from the experience of the past.

"Architecture, in fact, requires two different operations of the mind, —— the study and the application of precedent; application, because if all the masterpieces of the past were collected together in the brain of a single man, if he did not know how to avail himself of this knowledge, if he had no method to enable him to design properly by the aid of these masterpieces, he could only produce incongruous combinations of poor copies, mere limitations, which, in artistic value, would be far beneath the work of the barbarian who has no research, and has never studied the works of the past." [9]

Won't research stifle the levels of invention necessary to create new architectures? I think not, nor did Viollet-le-Duc:

"Enlarge your knowledge of precedent, form your judgment, learn to reason, and your faculty of invention will be increased."

The 20th-century architectural writer Karel Teige wrote that architecture should "transform itself into a new kind of science that would cancel out the old dualism between art form and technical form, not by denying art and embracing machine technology but by synthesizing ... technological, sociological and psychological factors of life." [10]

His is a notion whose time has finally arrived.

In imagining the Fourth Architecture there are parallels with Bucky Fuller's notion of "Design Science" and with Christopher Alexander's "A Pattern Language." Both are attempts to codify or systematize design through the lens of considering scientific or behavioral attributes of form.

Thus, we have directions to follow in creating a Fourth Architecture: utility, patterns of use, technologies – both new and old, forms and shapes that work.

So let us consider the basic shapes of building: the wall; the roof; the window; and the door – to learn what their natures tell us about why they "should" be shaped – and where those shapes are appropriate.

III. The Wall

In their respective natures, there are really only two kinds of wall – one is, *in* concept, *infinitely thin* and planar; the other forms plastic space and is therefore in concept *infinitely thick*.

While some will argue that a modeled (or warped – in plan) thin wall shapes space, a careful analysis of the balance between rhetoric (theory) and actuality shows that the modeled plane is primarily sculptural – form for form's sake, paid for by the Owner and inflicted on a pondering public.

Louis Kahn had this to say about walls:

"Now a word about inspired technology. The wall did well for humanity. The wall enclosed us for a long time until the man behind it, feeling a new freedom, wanted to look out. He hammered away to make an opening. The wall cried, 'What are you doing to me? I have protected you. I made you feel secure – and now you put a hole through me!' and the man said, 'But I see wonderful things, and I want to look out. I appreciated your faithfulness but I feel time has brought change.'

"The wall was sad; the man realized something good. He visualized the opening as gracefully arched, glorifying the wall. The wall was pleased with its arch and the man carefully made a jamb and a sill trimmed with fine stone.

"The opening became part of the order of the wall. Consider the momentous event when the wall parted and the column became."[7]

A wall may be paper thin or massively thick; most walls fall somewhere in between, with thicknesses of 150 to 300 mm (6 to 12 inches.)

When walls are given shape, the gestural possibilities of shapes give rise to figurative comparisons in the minds of the observers. But walls can do more.

The Spirit of the Wall

Where walls have great thickness, the depth of the wall can contain spaces within it. It can be modeled to create plastic space – space that embraces a volume and creates a behavioral or psychological effect upon its occupants.

Piercing a thick wall is an act of *deliberate* architecture. This is to be noted as we create the Fourth Architecture.

But creating a wall of perceived thin-ness, taut and shimmering *might also* create a work of true architecture; but in either case there are architectural implications. Beyond mere form making there is the hope that the wall not only creates an architectural effect, but serves to enhance the quality of life within the space that has been enclosed. That it *works*.

We note that some of the earliest walls were no more than skins stretched over a wooden frame. The most evocative walls of non-Occidental architecture are found in the tradition of Japanese shoji panels, assembled of sheets of rice paper laid across finely crafted wooden frames and slats. And they *work*.

In Japanese traditional architecture the geometric basis for the size and proportion of individual rooms is determined by the width (about 3 feet) and proportion (1:2) of the   tatami mats that cover the floors of the   buildings – and the orientation and placement of areas are in accord with philosophical and religious cosmologies specific to Japan in the 17th century. So – for the designers of the Imperial Villa at Katsura, for instance, the shapes and forms have meaning. The spaces do more than merely enclose volume, they have processional importance; they have site-specific reasons for being. They *work*.

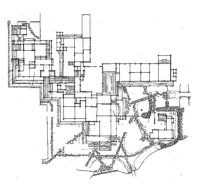

Or, as the British architect and writer Stephen Gardiner put it: "In Japanese art, space assumed a dominant role and its position was strengthened by Zen concepts."

This harkens to our earlier observations on the Hellenistic shift from a religion-based system of order, to a rational structural order.

Shoji panels at Katsura

We must note the influence of the Japanese house upon modern Western concepts of space, inspiring the flow of spaces in the   Prairie School houses of Frank Lloyd Wright and continuing on to ideas of "universal space" with ill-defined rooms, an idea that is pervasive up to our current era.

Wright's first glimpse of traditional Japanese architecture came at the 1893 Columbian Exposition when he encountered the Japanese Pavilion there.

Ho O Den (Phoenix Palace) Chicago, 1893

Wright carried forward the ideas of space flowing from room to room that he saw in the Japanese pavilion in his early "Prairie Style" houses. As an anodyne to the over-decorated, stuffy rooms of late 19th century western houses, the flowing arrangement of spaces seemed liberating, fresh and exciting.

Edwin Cheney House, 1903

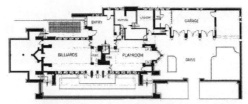

Plan of the Robie House, Chicago 1910

By the end of the 20th century this style of space planning had become a new hegemony, an approved style of architectural planning and design; in the hands of some designers, this space was thought of as "universal" in that it did not conform to individual room-space, but broke down the barriers between walled-in space and the "open plan."

But with this new tradition came a loss. We can do more than simply shape space. We can make forms that do more than simply *be*. And therein lies the source of our discontent.

Quality of Space Defined by Walls

In the days of antiquity, shaping of walls created spaces with purpose, with a reason for *being* enclosed. In our era, the configuration of walls is often a response to abstract rules imposed by society such as zoning ordinances, or building codes that require certain standards of structural firmness, or to the sculptural whims of a designer whose tools are the algorithms of a computer-generated script ("parametricism".)

Dear Richard,

Always great to get to talk.

Be well — Stay busy.

Best —
CB

Proceeds from the sale of this
Little Red Book go to the Associates' Fund
of the Cooper Union for the Advancement
of Science and Art, New York City.

Also, over several centuries, there has been the urge to de-solidify the wall, to render it as airy and light as a theatrical scrim, transparent and floating, defying the realities of gravity, of weather; creating a gossamer web, or a building-sized soap bubble. This was significantly driven forward by the new technology of structural iron, and continuing improvements in glass strength.

This de-materialization is one hallmark of the Third Architecture, otherwise known as "Modernism."

Increasingly larger panes of glass supported by a supple grid of iron became a style unto themselves – although the obvious references to the appearance of the greenhouse, which had been the province of princes and kings – allowing oranges and lemons to be cultivated in the long nights of northern European winter – disappears over the decades.

Two leading figures in the development of the glass house were Joseph Paxton, a renowned gardener whose gigantic greenhouse known as The Crystal Palace enclosed an entire international exposition in 1851; and a century later, R. Buckminster Fuller, inventor of the geodesic dome. What I find parallel in these examples is that the structural frame is *the* æsthetic expression, and the glazing merely an enclosing membrane, spanning between structural elements.

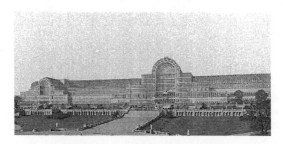

Crystal Palace, Hyde Park, London

Paxton's 1851 Crystal Palace and Fuller's 1967 bio-dome additionally share in each having had technologically advanced environmental systems for modulating heat and ventilation.

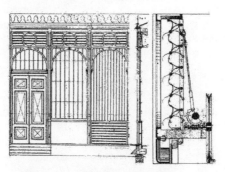

*The Crystal Palace ventilation system
Elevation and section.*

At the Crystal Palace sinusoidal-section louvers were mechanically linked and were manually operated by a corps of Royal Army sappers for ventilation.

44

Additionally – and of note from a technological point of view – the great greenhouse was air-conditioned! An evaporative cooling system of canvas panels, kept moist with water by the operating engineers (again, Royal Army sappers) maintained interior temperatures within two degrees Fahrenheit of the outside.

After the 1851 Exhibition the Crystal Palace was removed from it original site in Hyde Park, and re-erected with five stories, as seen here, using the original components.

These works blend the nature of roof and wall, as they both wrap space in all three axes, the x- y- and z-, but common to both is that they enclosed enormous volumes of space and remain remarkable engineering examples. But their utility is limited to merely the enclosing of large quantities of space. In that way they have much in common with the "universal space" described by enclosure of the modern glass house.

Æsthetically, two major proponents of the glass house genre – Ludwig Mies van der Rohe and his colleague Philip Johnson – are notable particularly for the popularization of a specific prototype to the use of glass walls, held separate from structure, true curtains, wholly independent of the building's structure.

The German architect and former Bauhaus director Mies, in his design for Dr Edith Farnsworth's house in Plano, Illinois (1945 – 51); his Crown Hall at the Illinois Institute of Technology in Chicago (1956); and architect Philip Johnson's own Glass House in New Canaan, Connecticut (1949) are the prime examples of the glass house experiment.

Farnsworth House, Plano, Illinois

The Glass House, New Canaan, Connecticut

Crown Hall, Chicago

All these buildings share the characteristic of having walls that have no shape – they describe an orthogonal resection of space, the fundamental idea being that the exterior and interior zones are basically identical. By the happenstance of the existence of the glass plane, interior space may be imagined to flow, uninterrupted in unity with the landscape otherwise set apart by the transparent curtain of glass. Draperies, if absolutely necessary (and it seems that Mies, for one, had a particular distaste for window coverings, or even for operable windows – much to the dismay of his client and one-time lover, Dr. Edith Farnsworth – who unsuccessfully sued her architect over a substantial litany of complaints) are the only element that definitively marks off "interior" from exterior in a glass house.

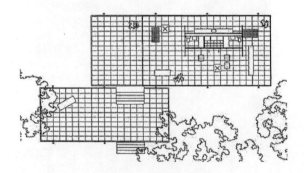

Farnsworth House Plan

Therefore, the universal space of the glass house, being essentially an expression of "nowhere-ness" makes for awkward patterns of use. The space extending beyond groupings of furniture (q.v: Johnson) could be infinite; spaces within the space are certainly possible – in Johnson's Glass House the kitchen is reduced to a pair of rectangular solids that just *happen* to be assemblies of residential appliances. The Farnsworth kitchen is an array of cabinetry along the back side of a fat wall that floats in the universal space of the house's pavilion-like enclosure.

Thus, it is not the walls of the glass house that make space, it is the composition of elements floating in the universal space within the arbitrary limits of the glass enclosure that create any denotative or perceptible aspects we think of as space. By extension, one imagines that the act of putting on a hat creates for the human being a building, and under its brim, a space. If we imagine for a moment that this is true, it is purely mental space – which is exactly what universal space represents: a mental construct, an idea of space, a system in which anything – or nothing can be imagined to happen.

So the real downside of universal space is that it creates the opportunity for anything, or nothing, as a functionality – and therefore, being of nothing, is of and in itself, nothing. For it is walls that create space, in the interplay of light and dark, illumination and shadow.

Seagram Building, New York City – Mies van der Rohe and Philip Johnson, Architects

Before moving on to other concepts of walls, I should freely admit that the curtain wall begs the question of the concept of window – that by making the entirety of a wall, in essence, one continuous window, the specificity of a window – framing a view, for instance – is lost. Where all of the *wall* is *window* there becomes a condition of there being neither wall nor window, merely a transparent curtain.

Utility

Where walls of glass become both enclosure and window, the architect has avoided making a distinction between wall and window; this is an act of architectural cowardice.

How does this transparent curtain work? It doesn't. It neither makes space as understood in a pre-modern sense of niches, naves, aisles, and secret cloisters; neither does it serve any utilitarian function beyond not-very-good thermal enclosure and keeping the rain out. It contains a volume of air, contains a volume of space that contains activities, but otherwise does nothing beyond containment. Its "work" capabilities are near to zero.

It can be argued, and many adherents to the cur-tain wall œsthetic will argue – if only for the sake of argument, because they are too lazy to address the artistic paucity of their adherence or because they have not really thought about this blind spot in any depth – that advanced, triple-glazed curtain wall can admit vast quantities of light while, at the same time, provide much better thermal perform-ance than, say, the original curtain walls of Mies' era.

But it can also be argued that highly insulated (q.v: *Passivhaus* ™) enclosures do a far better job of thermal performance and require the architect to actually make choices about where, and why, and how or in what fashion, to provide a building with windows.

In having to make choices, to make a positive deci-sion about form-making, lies the opportunity to make both a window that works towards a desired effect, and a wall, similarly, to productive purpose.

Antecedents

The Mass Wall of Antiquity: before the advent of the primary modern high-strength construction materials – rolled steel sections and steel-reinforced concrete – masonry walls and columns were the only practical structural support for floors and roofs of buildings larger than a house. Oh, yes, there were and still remain large stave churches, and Asian pagodas and temples of great antiquity that have wooden structure, but let us not quibble; let us look into the matter of mass walls.

The logic of economy might suggest that these heavy, labor-intensive walls should be as plain as possible, and indeed in the earliest architectures – Mesopotamian, western Mediterranean and pharonic Egyptian – this was generally the case. The mass wall, arguably, reached its finest expression beginning in the middle ages.

Let us consider the plan for the headquarters of the last of the Knights Templar, the Convento Cristo in Tomar, Portugal. The niches in the circular sanctuary – said to recall the organization of the Church of the Holy Sepulcher in Jerusalem – provide a modulation of space, as well as places in which to display relics, and to create altars.

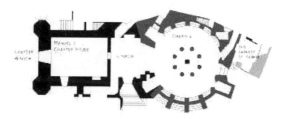

Convento Cristo

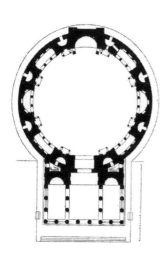

Similarly, the Pantheon, with its shrines to the many gods, allows a modulation of "plastic" space – space that is visually manipulated to impart a desired æsthetic effect. These walls work, in being both structural support and modulators of space.

It is, without a doubt, and believed by many, to be *the* greatest work of architecture in the extant world.

On this, the greatest room ever created, the architect Louis Kahn said:

"The structure of the room must be evident in the room itself. Structure, I believe is the giver of light. A square room asks for its own light to read the square. It would expect the light either from above or from its four sides as windows or entrances.

"Sensitive is the Pantheon. The non-directional room dedicated to all religions has its light only from the oculus above, placed to invest the room with inspired ritual without favoritism. The entrance door is its only impurity." [7]

The enduring fascination with and affection held by Western culture for our "gothic" and late-medieval (aka Renaissance, a revival of Hellenistic Roman antiquity) architecture is the plastic, i.e.: modulated, formation of space that delights the eye and enlivens the acoustic environment. So – by this metric such mass walls can be thought of as *working* to an æsthetic standard.

But there is more at work in mass wall construction.

Mass walls have thermal inertia – maintaining and containing warmth and coolness; creating the opportunity for spaces carved from within the depth of the wall (see plans above – the niches in both the Pantheon and Templar church.)

They are architecture, these walls, even when in a ruinous state. In such a state, says Kahn, they are liberated from use and can speak to us of their pure form and of how they were built – and possibly why:

"A building being built is not yet in servitude. It is so anxious to be that no grass can grow under its feet, so high is the spirit of wanting to be. When it is in service and finished, the building wants to say, 'Look, I want to tell you about the way I was made.' Nobody listens. But when the building is a ruin and free of servitude, the spirit emerges telling of the marvel that a building was made."[7]

We cannot, of course, leave the topic of the mass wall, or the conceptually infinitely-thick wall without a passing glance at Corbusier's chapel at Ronchamp. The thickness of the walls both cool the interior space and creates plastic space. In the hands of a master architect, sculptural effect can be authentically architectural.

Unintended Consequences

A recently-completed mass wall that serves a purpose not intended, with accidental characteristics that have been and continue to be the source of misery for its manifold users is a megastructure that was built as a dormitory at MIT by New York architect Steven Holl.

This is Simmons Hall, with a reinforced concrete wall that works very well – as a Faraday cage. Its relentless grid of 2' x 2' (600 x 600mm) steel windows form a conductive net that effectively blocks the passage of electromagnetic waves – outside to inside, and vice versa.

A dorm with no cell service is a disaster for students in the 21st century. So: not a very utilitarian form – except, *possibly*, a very effective form for the walls of an *embassy*, where blocking electromagnetic eavesdropping is always a matter of paramount concern.

But here, where the program is to house students of a technical university, this formal experiment is nothing short of an unmitigated disaster. And the failure of the architect is simply this: the failure – either by unwillingness to consider technology, or an ignorance of the physics and engineering at play.

Whether architects are masters of all aspects of the built environment, or are merely decorators, is easily resolved in this case. For this building is an excellent example of how "art" gets in the way of quality of life, an inconvenient introduction of use*less*ness.

Poor MIT.

Intended Consequences of a Wall that Works

This wall of prismatic elements – providing enhanced daylight harvesting while focusing daylight more efficiently on an array of photovoltaic cells – is from a proposed scheme for the Fashion Institute of Technology, New York City, by the New York Architects SHoP.

The system, "The HeliOptix Integrated Concentrating Solar Façade" was invented by Anna Dyson, Michael Jensen, and Peter Stark of the Center for Architecture Science and Ecology.

Each clear pyramid, less than a foot square, has a lens to focus sunlight onto a PV cell; the pyramidal modules rotate to track the sun. Pumped water keeps the cells cool to maximize efficiency, capturing waste heat for uses such as domestic hot water.

This, then, is a wall the shape of which is completely and exclusively the result of its intended function. It is a wall that *works*. It is, definitely, of the Fourth Architecture.

IV. The Roof

> There are really only two reasons for a building to have a roof: to keep weather out, and to keep interior atmosphere in. *Any other use of a roof is architecturally illegitimate.*

Without a critical assessment of *why* anything should have a shape, we have no basis for considering whether it is any good or not, for without reason we are left with pure opinion – pure formalism.

Speaking of formalism, here's the Sydney Opera House, by Jørn Utzon:

Why are the roofs shaped as they are?

Pure formalism.

Selection of this scheme was by juried competition. Here's what Frank Lloyd Wright had to say about that process:

"*The conditioned mind will learn by comparison. The enlightened mind will learn by analysis. So that's the evil done by a competition, like this one, where you judge – get a few – five or six young architects, who premiated this design for its sheer novelty without thinking, couldn't have analyzed the thing because it has nothing to do with opera. It has nothing to do with architecture.*

"*It's not a building. It's a construction of folded paper, or blown up with some kind of fabric and it has no relation to the plan – and it's a very bad plan for opera. Isn't it "art for art's sake" coming in again?*

"*The caprice of personal idiosyncrasy takes the place of thought? Seems we're going along in that direction with a little group that think that a twist, or some idiosyncratic expression of form is artistic. Well it has been, in its day; that's when we had I'Art Nouveau – that's when we had all this movement that was to me reprehensible, and is still. So I felt that this was a terrible thing to foist upon the people of Australia.*"[11]

Let us now consider the mushroom-like roof at a funicular station in Innsbruck, Austria – the Hunger-burgbahn–Bergstation, designed by Zaha Hadid, which we have previously seen. It is a sculptural form that draws the eye, but does not form space.

It *somewhat* shelters the entrance to the station, although its shape begs questions about shelter from the weather. We find no expression of the structure, no inkling of what the structure *is* at all. Instead what we have is mysterious structure clad in "Smurf" æsthetic.

The cladding is problematic, in that it could be con-structed of porcelain-covered aluminum, or glossy plastic, or even a temporary installation in resin-coated papier maché. Why is the Hungerburgbahn roof so *clumsy* as compared with the Art Nouveau Métro canopies of Hector Guimard?

Scale and articulation. Does this Métro canopy shape space? No. But does it articulate an "event" – most certainly! However, the Hungerburgbahn also does this. What, then, are defining differences between Hadid's and Guimard's canopies?

In Guimard, the use of the materials chosen – cast iron and glass – are true to the capabilities of their structural abilities.

Where Guimard's canopy calls to mind an up-springing of branches, or of fern fronds, either a delightful token of having been returned to the surface after our subterranean journey, or a reminder that after our trip on Le Métro we will be returned to the verdant surface, Hadid's organic expression evocative of – a gigantic fungus – is grossly problematic. "*De gustibus non disputatum est*" has never been more apt.

As Guimard's shape-making has *reason*, it therefore "works" on both a structural and an æsthetic level that far surpasses that of Hadid's promethean mushroom. Or perhaps – is the Hungerburgbahn – Bergstation canopy a *joke*? If so, at whose expense? To what end?

Now let us get down to some serious enquiry into shapes that work, and how they do so – or in the case of the *flat roof* – don't really work all that well.

The most pervasive form of the modernist hegemony of style is the flat roof. It derives from mud houses of both the Levantine and American Southwest.

Both of these climates are dry and a sun-baked structure with a flat roof is both appropriate and to a certain extent expedient. In either case, however, the flat roof does nothing to provide for air circulation in the rooms being sheltered, because the constant horizontal plane thus established creates no vertical variation, upon which convective air currents rely for maximal usefulness in carrying heat upwards, and promoting the infiltration of cooler air from below.

This is one of the reasons that ground floor stories in dwellings and commercial buildings of recent history (18th through early 20th century) have elevated ceilings; being in closest proximity to the heat-absorbing pavements of the adjacent site they gain radiant heat from their surrounding.

With a tall ceiling, accumulated heat can rise far above the head level of the occupants, and be carried out of the structure through the open sashes of high windows. (But let us not be distracted by the attractive prospect of beautiful, high windows; not just yet.)

In defense of the flat roof, it may be pointed out that it does not "waste space." Now, in a commercial sense, where additional enclosed volume may be viewed as an extravagance to be meted out with great economy and circumspection, this may be a virtue. However, when we consider the enduring expense of mechanical ventilation and cooling required in low-ceilinged spaces as compared with the "free" cooling of a high ceiling that relies upon natural phenomena, the argument becomes somewhat sketchy.

What a flat roof *does* provide is a level surface for the various mechanical appurtenances necessary in a high-rise structure: cooling towers, water tanks, window washing rigs, and maintenance scaffolding davits.

The recent phenomenon of attempting to remediate the undesirable heat gain on flat roofs of dark color by covering them with vegetative beds ("green roofs") notwithstanding, there is little reason for a roof to be flat other than from shear economics of construction. It's cheaper than a roof with a shape, but is generally useless for any purpose other than a mounting surface for equipment.

Other shapes of roof include the shed; the gable; the vaulted, arched roof; the rotated arch, or dome; the hip roof; the "Mansart", gambrel; and the pyramid.

Oh, and also the warped parametric artistic roof – the tormented fish-shaped or exploded beer can roof on any of many Frank Gehry or Zaha Hadid projects.

Gehry Partners at Bard College.
Sic transit gloria mundi.

Some technical talk

The flat ceiling and flat roof limit our expected daylight "throw" to about 15 feet; the slanted ceiling and/or shed roof can improve upon that.

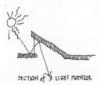

SECTION of A LIGHT MONITOR

In artists' studios and industrial buildings of the 19th and early 20th centuries we see a variant of the shed in the form of repeating light "monitors." This shape *works*.

The Gable Roof, Exalted

A GABLE ROOF

So what does the gable roof *do*? It sheds water left and right, and it creates an attic space of limited usefulness. As a ceiling, its usefulness for spreading daylight is about nil – *unless* in an adjacent wall there is a high window.

One drawback of the gable is the requisite lateral bracing element.

The Gothic solved this structural challenge to great effect with its flying buttresses – or, as in the case at Wells Cathedral (at right) with an inverted arch at the crossing.

A convenient opportunity for some artful form-making! But here, the art of the form doesn't get in the way of its usefulness. It enhances it.

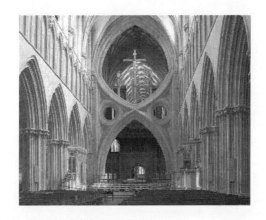

Although of the Gothic – the Second Architecture, with its structural logic – it can *arguably* be said are also elements of the Fourth Architecture, as well.

A result of the "Design Science" thinking of Bucky Fuller is a roof he designed that solves a very pressing technical challenge – it naturally cools the house, for as we know, heating is relatively easy – in much of North America, it's *cooling* that is the greater energy challenge.

This is the Dymaxion "Wichita"House, with a roof that is modeled on the traditional American barn ventilator.

It looks strange to our eyes, long accustomed to the conventional shapes of tradition; but once we understand the reason for its shape – it is beautiful.

Of all the Shapes that Work, perhaps the most compelling, and not at all unlike the Dymaxion roof is the ancient Persian windcatcher – or *shish-khan*.

Persian windcatcher towers

Ideal for dry climates, windcatchers have been used in recent times at the Visitors Center at Zion National Park, in Utah:

But before we leave this topic, there is one additional and notable example of the Shape of Roofs that Work –

Primary school in Gando, Burkina Faso – by
Diébédo Francis Kéré, 2001

The school is constructed of rammed earth bricks, as is the inner arched roof. The outer roof shields the inner roof from insolation – solar loading – whilst allowing cooling breezes to flow over the mass of the inner roof.

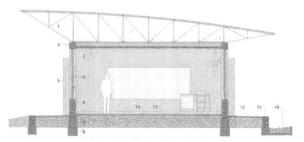

Section showing the mass roof
enclosing the classroom space,
air space between it and the
airfoil-like outer roof.

These are truly Shapes that Work.

V. The Window

There are only three reasons to create a window: to allow daylight to enter; to facilitate ventilation; and to frame a view – either of an external vista or becoming, in and of itself a view.

Geodesic "Bio-dome" of Expo '67 – Montreal
Fuller and Sadao

Is this dome all window, or is it all wall – or both? Fuller's *bio-dome* – at Montreal, for Expo 67, has a shape that, of course, expresses its structural function. Aside from enclosing a volume it doesn't *do* much more.

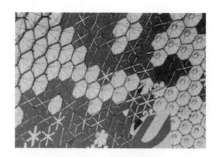

The Expo 67 dome was shaded by an array of metalized fabric blinds (above) that opened and closed according to the solar angle – and which could also be opened in decorative sequences as entertainment. These were controlled by a system of sensors, drive motors, and a data processing system – no small feat in the pre-PC days of the mid-20th century, when computers required punched cards for data input.

Here are some windows which, despite their unique stylistic flourishes, satisfy all the criteria for windows:

Designed by Antoni Gaudi, in Barcelona – these admit a (street) view at the lower sash; they allow ventilation; and in and of themselves become *the*

view at the upper clerestory sash. They also spread colored light into the rooms within by means of the art glass in that upper sash.

Hence, these windows satisfy the fundamentals of window *nature*, and may be thought of as an example of the Fourth Architecture.

Here (above) are more windows of the Fourth Architecture, at the north façade of the Whitney Museum, Marcel Breuer architect. They frame a view from the galleries towards the decidedly unmodern streetscape of Madison Avenue, as well admitting daylight.

An example of fairly recent windows that *work* can be seen at the curtainwall of Jean Nouvel's *Institut* du *Monde Arabe*, circa 1997, in Paris.

These nested arrays of irises open and close according to sunlight conditions, moderating daylight as well as becoming decorative view elements in and of themselves. A drawback to these automaton eyes – which remind me of E.T.A. Hoffman's *Olympia* – the goddess robot doll – is that often the control electronics do not work; over-reliance on gadgetry is a failure of buildings that aspire to be of the Fourth Architecture.

On the elemental level, and in the spirit of what is old is new again, is the *jalousie* window; it provides daylight and facilitates ventilation. But – you may say, it is an ugly window that disrupts view. Ah, but beauty is subjective, and the jalousie's utility cannot be disputed.

Bay window glazed with jalousies at the Conklin & Rossant designed Butterfield House, 1962 – New York City

William Conklin, the American architect and co-designer of the building with the above-referenced jalousie windows, tells us that Walter Gropius (under whom he studied at Harvard) believed the ribbon window to be more "democratic;" that individual windows favored some locations within a building at the expense of other locations not adjacent to a window.

The ribbon window provides views from *all* areas inside.

While this is pragmatically true, the ribbon windows at, for example, the 1927 Weißenhof Siedlung, are unremarkable and banal. They don't seem to *do anything*. They simply *are*, seen from the vantage point of 90 years.

Ribbon windows at Weißenhofsiedlung – near Stuttgart

Where there is *all* view, there is *no* view, because the view is not framed by intention.

Where walls of glass become both enclosure and window, the architect has avoided making a distinction of any of these three functions, and commits an act of architectural cowardice. Where ribbons windows become a slash across the structural integrity of the wall both the visual integrity of the wall and the distinction of the window are lost.

Perhaps this made perfect sense in the early 20th century, when viewing the ruins of the 19th century wrought by the horrors of the Great War – the war to end all wars.

But to us, inured to both the horrid ruins of war and equally inured to the romantic notions of war-wrought ruins as *mementi mori* – this is insufficient; we require better forms, shapes, and expressions.

We require Shapes that Work.

VI. The Door

Doors keep things and people separated – in or out. There is no other reason for them to exist.

Formally speaking, doors have to express one of two goals: to be sympathetic to (and accommodate) the scale of the person who will pass through it – as a facilitator of respect for personal dignity; or, by massive over-scale and size, to suppress personal dignity.

In that historical period between the diminishment of the Gothic, (Second Architecture,) and the reinterpretation of the First Architecture – the so-called Renaissance, Mannerist and Rococo eras – manipulation of scale became a favorite trope of architects. The supposed majesty of a potentate or religious/civil regime was expressed by means of the gigantic door.

Consider the following image, then: this is the entrance portal to the Apostolic Palace of the Pope, at the Vatican. The "renaissance" penchant for antique formalism extends beyond the architecture; to this day, the Swiss mercenaries who guard the Pope wear uniforms believed to have been designed by Michelangelo.

Of course, this Vatican door has antecedents in the
Roman – *First* Architecture. But that predecessor
was sized for *gods* – as we see in the example of
the entrance to the Pantheon.

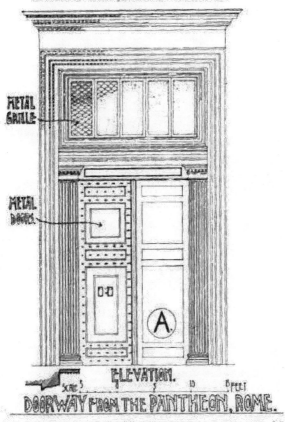

ROMAN DOORWAYS.

METAL GRILLE.

METAL DOORS.

ELEVATION.

SCALE 5 0 5 10 15 FEET

DOORWAY FROM THE PANTHEON, ROME.

Doors can also be made to be uncomfortably low –
as a defensive measure. Consider this very low door
from a reconstructed Viking fortress. Anyone, friend
or foe, must bend low, lowering one's head (and
neck) upon crossing the threshold.

A notable exception to the Western convention of
"the door" can be found in the traditional Japanese house, which has *no* doors. Walls are the
doors, and are composed of panels that slide,
modifying the flow and shape of space.

VIII. Last Thoughts

Consider the architectural forms of Dubuffet sculptures; you can parse all the words you like – in architectural parlance – but that does not make them architecture.

So: even *if* a form is monumental, structural, has elegance, scale and wit ———

it's not architecture.

Like it as much as you will, the sculpture of Jean Dubuffet – perhaps the most architectural of all sculptors – is not architecture.

Analogously, the sculptural qualities of so-called Parametricism, therefore, may not reach the level of architecture, and therefore, according to Hejduk's dictum may only be *building*. Or sculpture.

It is for you to decide.

———————————————

Codicil

The Basic Rights and Rules of Dwelling

The Rights and Rules of Dwelling were written by Curtis B Wayne in 2012 for discussion by members of The Congress of Residential Architecture at their annual convention in Chicago.
www.CORArchitecture.org

The Rights

I. Freedom from Interference:

> *Every dwelling shall provide isolation be-tween neighbors and neighborhood.*
>
> *The dwelling entrance shall afford privacy, in accord with the United Nations Universal Declaration of Human Rights, Article 13: "(1) Everyone has the right to freedom of movement and residence"*
>
> *Further to this Right is the specter of expanded surveillance of all members of society by military and civilian intelligence-gathering organizations. The mere fact of surveillance diminishes the enjoyment of Dwelling in a free and undisturbed state of being.*

II. Establishment of Personal Space:

> *Every person shall a space to him/herself; a shared bedroom does not suffice.*

> *Such a space may be an alcove with a drape, a corner of a garage, a niche off of a kitchen, or a contained room, but in all cases shall be visually separated from common-use spaces.*

III. Access to the Sky:

> *No less than one Juliet balcony per dwelling, or one garden room, one patio, one semi-enclosed deck*

IV. Availability of Daylight:

> *Every occupiable space shall be illuminated by daylight to the greatest extent feasible. Measures shall be taken by the architect to ensure this Right.*

> *Further to this Right, artificial illumination shall be integrated with daylight sources, so that no harsh contrasts are created, day or night whilst within the Dwelling.*

V. Promotion of Economy:

The life-cycle of a Dwelling far exceeds the life expectancy of its original owner. It is the duty of the Designer to incorporate as great a level of energy efficiency in the Dwelling as feasible – as an obligation to the greater good of the Community.

VI. Promotion of Efficiency:

Convenience shall be regarded as more than a nicety. Kitchens, bathing rooms, sleeping rooms and common rooms shall be efficiently arranged and ergonomically correct.

The Rules

1. The Rule of Entering:

No dwelling shall be entered directly from the outside.

2. The Rule of Size: enough but not too much:

No less than 500 sq ft per person, no more than 1,500.

3. The Rule of Ventilation:

Every sleeping space shall have at least two ventilating exposures.

4. The Rule of bath light and ventilation:

> *Every bathing room shall have a window.*

5. The Rule of View:

> *Windows without a view shall have ornamental glazing.*

6. The Rule of Light and Material:

> *Materials and finishes shall play well with sunlight.*

7. The Rule of Roofs:

> *Roofs shall respect the site climate; no flat roofs in climates where it snows or rains extensively.*

> *No roof – excepting a flat roof – shall have gutters, nor leaders.*

8. The Rule of the Vertical:

> *Ground floor ceilings shall be no less than 9 feet, nor higher than 11 feet.*

9. The Rule of Ascending:

No stair between dwelling levels shall have a straight run;

All stairs shall have at least one landing. Preferably the landing shall have a seating place and a window.

10. The Rule of the Right Window:

Some windows are for ventilation, some for daylight, and some for view.

The purpose of a window should be self-evident, and its shape should be optimized for its differentiation and purpose.

11. The Rule of Storage

For each person living in the dwelling, there shall be no less than 10 linear feet of closet space at least 25" deep, with 10 linear feet of hang rod and 10 linear feet of 12" deep shelving above the rod.

Clothing drawers and cabinets shall be incorporated into the thickness of walls to obviate moveable dressers and miscellaneous storage furniture.

Notes:

Foreword:

Frank Lloyd Wright, interview on WNYC radio, 1957
http://www.wnyc.org/blogs/neh-preservation-project/2013/feb/25/frank-lloyd-wright/#commentlist
R. Buckminster fuller quotation: Buckminster Fuller Institute
http://www.bfl.org/

(1)   R. Buckminster Fuller, loc. cit.
(2)   *Education of an Architect* Video, Michael Blackwood Productions, no date. Available for sale at:
http://www.michaelblackwoodproductions.com/archs_cooperunion.php
Excerpted at: http://www.youtube.com/watch?v=chEfhs-kEXQ
(3)   David Chipperfield, RIBA. "Chipperfield: More Community" Interview by Julie Iovine, *Il Giornale dell'Architettura with The Architect's Newspaper*, 27 August 2012, page 6, in which he is quoted as saying: "Architecture has to have meaning, not just novelty. The biggest ambition can't be just to be different. When we only talk about what architecture looks like, its colour or what's in the lobby we are just becoming decorators."
http://issuu.com/archpaper/docs/biennale_27_agosto/7
(4)   A. Tzonis and L. Lefaivre "The Question of Autonomy in Architecture" *Harvard Architectural Review 3*, Harvard University Graduate School of Design, 1984.
http://tzonis.com/dks/dks/publications/online%20publications/1984-HAR-The%20Question%20of%20Autonomy.htm
(5)   *Discourses on Architecture*, Eugène Emmanuel Viollet-le-Duc, Tr. by, with an introductory Essay by Henry Van Brunt, James R. Osgood and Company, Boston, 1875. Available on Google Books.
(6)   "The Tall Office Building, Artistically Considered," *Lippincott's Monthly Magazine, a Popular Journal of General Literature, Science, and Politics. Volume LVII, Page 408*
http://babel.hathitrust.org/cgi/pt?id=uc1.b5213377;seq=423;view=1up;num=403
(7)   Louis I. Kahn, 1971 American Institute of Architects Gold Medal Acceptance Speech, Detroit, MI June 24, 1971
(8)   Chipperfield, loc. cit.
(9)   Viollet-le-Duc, loc. cit.
(10)   *The Minimum Dwelling* Karel Teige, Tr. by Eric Dluhosch, MIT Press
(11)   Frank Lloyd Wright, loc. cit.

Credits:

Page 10. Illustration *from A History of Architecture on the Comparative Method*, Sir Bannister Fletcher, 1890

Page 11. Salisbury Cathedral Chapter House
www.salisburycathedral.co.uk/img/images/history.chapterhouse.jpg

Page 12. Condominiums on Astor Place, New York City. Gwathmey Siegel Architects.
http://rrscaffold.com/uploads/images/Gallery/Projects/Project1/astor-place---final-demo-030.jpg

Page 14. New Academic Building, The Cooper Union, New York City. Morphosis Architects, designers; Gruzen Samton Executive Architects
http://blog.archpaper.com/wordpress/wp-content/uploads/2011/10/41_cooper_square_05.jpg

Page 15. Glaxo Wellcome Building, Greenford, UK RMJM Architects
http://www.murdochltd.com/projects/propics/glaxo/glaxo-1.jpg

Pages 16 – 17 Chicago "A Century of Progress" World's Fair, 1934 – 35 Souvenir Booklet. Collection of the author.

Page 18. View of Counter Space: Design and the Modern Kitchen. The Museum of Modern Art, New York, 2009. Photo by Jonathan Muzikar

Pages 19 – 20. Helicon Building, London. Sheppard Robson Architects
www.sheppardrobson.com/uploads/projects/Helicon/Helicon1.jpg
www.sheppardrobson.com/uploads/projects/Helicon/Helicon3.jpg
www.skyscrapernews.com/images/pics/4676TheHelicon_pic4.jpg

Page 21. Ceiling of Sir John Soane's Breakfast Room
http://www.nycinteriordesign.com/2010/09/page/2/#

Page 22. Hungerburg Bergstation – Zaha Hadid Architects
http://commons.wikimedia.org/wiki/File:Hungerburgbahn-Bergstation.JPG   Photo by Hakelar

Page 31. King Abdullah Petroleum Studies and Research Center (KAP-SARC) Zaha Hadid Architects www.zaha-hadid.com

Page 34. Illustration from Dictionnaire raisonné de l'architecture française *du XIe au XVIe siècle* (1875). Eugène Emmanuel Viollet-*le*-Duc

Page 39. Plan of Imperial Villa at Katsura, 17th century
http://www.greatbuildings.com/cgi-bin/gbc-
drawing.cgi/Imperial_Villa_Katsura.html/Katsura_Plan.jpg

Page 40. Interior of Shokin-tei, Katsura.
Photo by Raphael Azevedo Franca
http://upload.wikimedia.org/wikipedia/commons/0/09/Shokin-tei.jpg

Page 41, top. Ho O Den. Photo from Columbian Exposition Souvenir
Handbook. Collection of the author.

Page 41. middle. Edward Cheney House – Frank Lloyd Wright Architect
http://upload.wikimedia.org/wikipedia/commons/1/1e/2010-04-
10_3000x2000_oakpark_edwin_h_cheney_house.jpg
Photo by J. Crocker

Page 42. Plan of Robie House – Frank Lloyd Wright Architect
http://data.greatbuildings.com/gbc/drawings/Robie_Plan_2.jpg

Pages 44 – 46. Crystal Palace. Contemporary Souvenir Drawings and
Photographs, 1851.

Page 47, top. Farnsworth House, Mies van der Rohe Architect
Library of Congress, Prints and Photographs Division, Historic American
Buildings Survey, HABS: ILL,47-PLAN.V,1-9

Page 47, middle. The Glass House, Philip Johnson Architect
Still from *Points on a Line*, Film by Sarah Morris, 2009
http://upload.wikimedia.org/wikipedia/en/9/9b/Points_on_a_Line%2C_
Glass_House.jpg

Page 47, bottom. Crown Hall, Mies van der Rohe Architect
http://upload.wikimedia.org/wikipedia/commons/d/d8/Crown_Hall_so
uth.jpg   Photo by Jenn22356

Page 48. Plan of Farnsworth House, Mies van der Rohe Architect
www.architakes.com/wp-content/uploads/2009/10/PLANS1.jpg

Page 58. West elevation of Seagram Building, Mies van der Rohe Architect www.flickr.com/photos/dandeluca Photo by dandeluca

Page 53, top. Plan of Convento de Cristo, Tomar PT.
http://upload.wikimedia.org/wikipedia/commons/e/e5/TomarChurchPl
anCC3.jpg

Page 53, middle. Plan of the Pantheon. *Kirchliche Baukunst des Abend-landes.* Georg Dehio/Gustav von Bezold, Stuttgart: Verlag der Cotta'schen Buchhandlung 1887-1901, Plate No. 1.
http://upload.wikimedia.org/wikipedia/commons/6/67/Dehio_1_Pantheon_Floor_plan.jpg

Page 55. Plan of Chapelle Notre-Dame-du-Haut de Ronchamp
Le Corbusier Architect – *Oeuvre complete*

Page 56. Simmons Hall, MIT. Steven Holl Architect
http://upload.wikimedia.org/wikipedia/commons/6/6b/Simmons_Hall%2C_MIT%2C_Cambridge%2C_Massachusetts.JPG Photo by Daderot

Page 58. FIT project. HeliOptix Integrated Concentrating Solar Façade
SHoP Architects
http://www.helioptix.com/images/FIT_HeliOptixWall.jpg

Page 58. Photo by Kevin Rivoli, AP.
http://www.nbcnews.com/id/35726826/ns/us_news-environment/t/solar-power-future-glass-pyramids/#.UcNoC5zpxCl

Page 60. Sydney Opera House, Jørn Utzon Architect
http://upload.wikimedia.org/wikipedia/commons/4/40/Sydney_Opera_House_Sails.jpg

Page 62. Canopy of Hungerburg Bergstation, Zaha Hadid Architects
http://commons.wikimedia.org/wiki/File:Hungerburgbahn-Bergstation.JPG
Photo by Hakelar

Page 63. Metro Entrance Canopy. Photo by the author

Page 66. The Richard B. *Fisher Center* for the Performing Arts at Bard College. Gehry Partners Architects
http://upload.wikimedia.org/wikipedia/commons/2/20/Bard_College_Fisher_Center_front_view.jpg Photo by Daniel Case

Page 68, top. Wells Cathedral Strainer Arches
http://upload.wikimedia.org/wikipedia/commons/3/36/Wells_St_Andrews_Cross_arches.JPG Photo by Adrian Pingstone

Page 68, bottom. Dymaxion "Wichita" House, R. Buckminster Fuller, designer Photo of model Museum of Modern Art's "Home Delivery" pre-fab exhibit, 2008

Page 69, top. Iranian windcatcher
http://en.wikipedia.org/wiki/File:AbAnbarNain2.jpg

Page 69, bottom. Zion's national park visitor center windcatchers
http://stripedpot.com/wp-content/uploads/450visitors.jpg

Page 70. Primary school roof – elevation. Gando, Burkina Faso Diébédo
Francis Kéré, Architect
http://betterarchitecture.files.wordpress.com/2013/06/c2a9-francis-
kere.jpeg

Page 71, Primary school. Gando, Burkina Faso
http://betterarchitecture.files.wordpress.com/2013/06/1.jpg

Page 72. Biodome, R. Buckminster Fuller, designer and Shoji Sadao
Architect.
http://upload.wikimedia.org/wikipedia/commons/8/8c/Biosph%C3%A8r
e_Montr%C3%A9al.jpg
Photo by Cédric Thévenet

Page 73, top. Automated shades at Expo 67 Biodome. Fuller and Sadao
http://transformit.com/Portals/28522/images/USA21s.jpg

Page 73, bottom. Casa Mila, Barcelona. Antoni Gaudi Architect
Photo by MaryRebecca Hayden Taylor

Page 74, top. North Façade, Whitney Museum. Marcel Breuer Architect.
Photo by the author.

Page 74, bottom. Institut du Monde Arabe, Paris Jean Nouvel Architect
Photo by the author.

Page 75. Jalousie Bay Window, Butterfield House. Mayer Whittlesey &
Glass (William Conklin, James Rossant designers) Photo by the author.

Page 76. Weißenhofsiedlung. Pierre Jeanneret and le Corbusier
Architects
http://upload.wikimedia.org/wikipedia/commons/5/56/Weissenhof_Mie
s_1.jpg   Photo by shaqspeare

Page 79. Entrance to Apostolic Palace, The Vatican. Bernini (?)
http://upload.wikimedia.org/wikipedia/commons/6/67/Swiss_Guard_at
_the_Bronze_Door.jpg
Photo by Clayton Tang

Page 80. Illustration *from A History of Architecture on the Comparative Method*, Sir Bannister Fletcher, 1890.

Page 81. Viking fortress door
http://3.bp.blogspot.com/_ybSQeWxYLE0/TJT9tSaSMsI/AAAAAAAAKrg/ySXrUsTgljY/s1600/100_2936.JPG

Page 96. Photo by Will Colby. http://williamcolby.com/

Colophon

Cover design by Caitlin Everett, graphic artist
www.caitlineverett-art.net

Special thanks to my collaborators and supporters:

Guy Horton, architectural thinker and writer – who in-sisted that this "*crazy is good*" project was worthy. *Guy writes for Atlantic Cities, Metropolis, ArchDaily, and Archinect. Guy is a frequent co-host of the radio program on architecture and design "DnA" on KCRW, Santa Monica.*
http://archinect.com/people/cover/2283854/

Duo Dickinson – for comments and encouragement
Architect and author
http://savedbydesign.wordpress.com/

Graham McKay – for having vetted the text
Professor and blogger
http://misfitsarchitecture.com/

And to all my many professors and instructors without whose hectoring lo these many decades I would not have attempted this, my manifold thanks.

About the author

Curtis B Wayne is an architect and the creator of the architecture podcast "Burning Down the House" on the Heritage Radio Network and iTunes.

http://www.heritageradionetwork.com/programs/18-Burning-Down-The-House

Licensed and in practice for over thirty years, Curtis has designed buildings in various styles, but wishes for the Fourth Architecture to become *the* accepted non-style approach to buildings that raise the level of comfort, utility and beauty in our built landscape.

A native of Chicago, having publicly acknowledged his aversion to Midwestern winters, Curtis now resides and practices in New York City. He is a graduate of The Cooper Union for the   Advancement of Science and Art, New York City and of the Harvard Design School.   You   can   reach   Curtis   at cbwayne@post.harvard.edu

Postscript

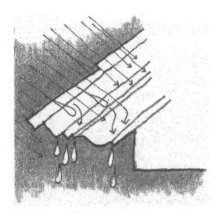

The historical *cyma recta* (*curved* and *squared*) moulding we encountered on the frontispiece *works* because its shapes wick away rain from the junction between the roof surface and its support.

Simple – and beautiful. And it works.

What do we learn from these analyses? That what a shape looks like may or may *not* add to its value. That a shape that works and is beautiful is to be desired above that which is merely beautiful

Thus, architecture cannot simply be what it *looks like*, but rather how it works to elevate the comfort, the convenience, and the happiness of the humans who encounter it. That is the Fourth Architecture.

Made in the USA
Charleston, SC
27 August 2013